MAGIC OF INDIA

Book inspired by my daughter, Siya. 💖

Go to our website, magicofindia.org
To hear the correct sound pronunciation of new words,
learn how to sing the Holi song and much more.

In this book you will find:

- 2 Fascinating stories on the origins of Holi.
- Learn new Indian words.
- Colourful and creative activity pages.
- The making of Holi colours.
- Holi festive food.
- A fun ride into how Holi is played in India and across the world.

By Geeta Srivastava, Teacher at Magic of India
Illustrated by Cameron Burns

Contributors: Siya Narayan, Victoria Brook & Rohit Prakash

Copyright ©2023 Magic of India
Magic of India
www.magicofindia.org

Published by
Magic of India, UK, London, NW6 1HS

Holi – the festival of colours
Celebrating Spring

Holi is a lively Indian festival that symbolizes all colours coming together in Spring to celebrate differences.

Holi is celebrated for two days. On the first day a bonfire is lit to celebrate the victory of good over evil.

The second day is filled with colours and festivities.

But what does the word Holi mean?

The word Holi comes from the word "hola" which means to offer gratitude for a good harvest season. This festival is full of fun and joy.

People gently throw and smear coloured powder on friends and family. Also in warmer places, they play with water sprays called Water sprays called "pich-kari".

'Holi Hai' means 'It is Holi'!

With colours flying in the air
Holi is a playful event.
As friends and family celebrate away
They sing together "Holi Hai!".

Do you know the story of how Holi started?

Legend has it that while Radha, Krishna's childhood friend, was fair-skinned,
Krishna was blessed with a unique blue skin tone.
It is said that blue signifies infinite powers.

One day, when little Krishna asked his mother why his skin was not the same colour as Radha's, she playfully told him to put some blue colour on Radha to match his skin tone. Krishna picked up on this fun idea and started smearing colour on Radha and all his friends. They all had a fun party and this tradition continues even today.

With coloured faces and happy smiles Krishna
and Radha played all day.

The festival of Holi brought them together
and colours blurred their differences away!

Why do we light a bonfire on the night before the Holi party?

This is the story of Prahalad and Holika.

Long ago there lived an evil king named Hiranyakashipu. His genius and cunning earned him a special blessing from the great lord, Brahma, Master of Creation.

What a long name! Can you pronounce it? Here is some help:

Hi – ran – y – ka – shi – pu

Hiranyakashipu was made immortal, meaning that could not be killed indoors or outdoors or at any time of the day or night.

No human or animal could harm him, even if they got into a fatal fight.

He could not be killed on Earth or in Space.

No weapon of destruction could hurt him.

With this power, he demanded every citizen in his kingdom to worship only HIM.

Hiranyakashipu's son, Prahalad, grew up in his mother's care with stories of good deeds of Lord Vishnu. Prahalad grew up to be a very kind and gentle boy. He was a big devotee of Lord Vishnu, the protector of the people. Prahalad did not worship his father. This made Hiranyakashipu so angry that he decided to kill his own son.

How do you say
Prahalad?
Pra - ha - lad

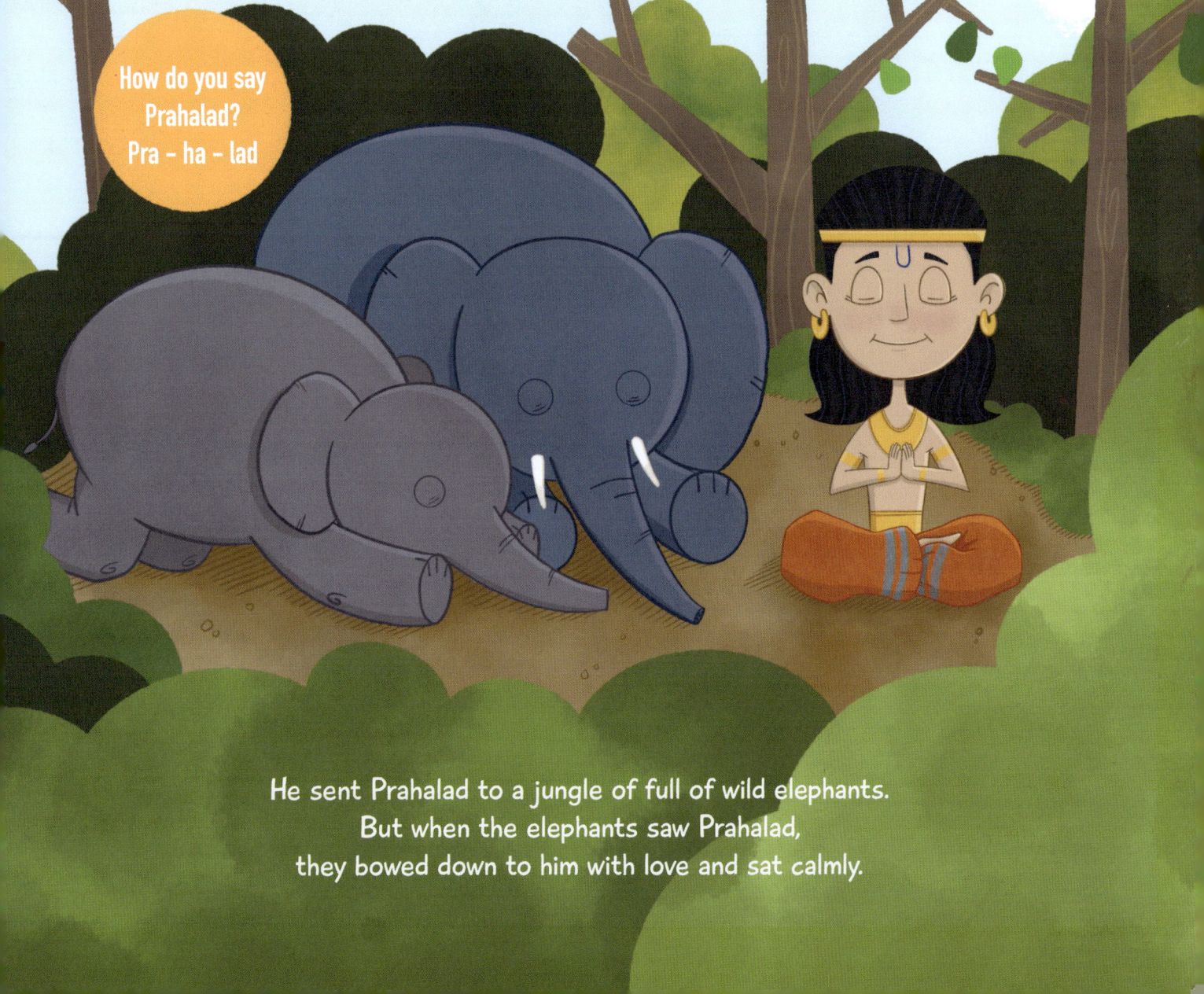

He sent Prahalad to a jungle of full of wild elephants.
But when the elephants saw Prahalad,
they bowed down to him with love and sat calmly.

His father then threw him in a jail, full of dangerous snakes, but not one snake harmed Prahalad.

He was taken by soldiers and thrown down a hill, but he was not hurt at all.

Vishnu cared for Prahalad, his loving disciple and protected him with a charming spell.

So finally, after all his attempts had failed, Hiranyakashipu asked his sister, Holika, for help.
Holika, who was blessed by Lord Brahma too, had a unique cloak that stopped her from being burned by fire! Wearing her magic cloak, she started a fire and sat in the flames with Prahalad on her lap. Holika thought that this would kill Prahalad and she would be safe.

But she was wrong.

The Gods did not like Holika using her powers for harming anyone and hence took away her magic power. Prahalad prayed to Lord Vishnu and, like magic, the cloak flew over Prahalad and he was saved while Holika was destroyed.

Hiranyakashipu was furious!
He demanded that Lord Vishnu show
himself and in anger, he struck a pillar
with his sword!

The pillar broke and with a thundering
sound emerged 'Narasimha', an avatar,
a new form of Lord Vishnu.

Narasimha is
pronounced,
Nara - sim - ha

Narasimha was half lion and half man.
He roared with fury and might.
He took the cruel King to the doorway.
Neither indoor nor outdoor.
It was twilight, neither day nor night.
Narasimha pulled the King on his lap.
So he was neither on Earth nor air.
He pierced him with his lion claws
The demon king died in despair.

Prahalad's belief in Lord Vishnu was rewarded and, once again, the world was saved from a cruel, tyrant King. Prahalad grew up to become a very wise and caring ruler.

And that's why we light the bonfire!

The first celebration takes place the night before with the lighting of a bonfire. This signifies the victory over evil of Holika and Hiranyakashipu. This ritual known as "Holika Dahan" falls on the night of the full moon (Purnima in Hindi), usually in the month of March (Phalguna).

Phalguna is pronounced, Phal – gu – na

How do you say Purnima? Pu – r – ni – ma

What happens at Holika Dahan?

Everyone gathers to sing and dance around the bonfire. As the bonfire rages, people throw grains, popcorn, b-ta-sha (sweet candy), coconut and chickpeas into the burning flame and put the ash on their foreheads as a blessing.

This evening is also known as "Choti Holi".

Choti means: small

Full Moon

Holi – A new beginning!

Holi is celebrated to mark the arrival of Spring, after a long cold winter.
Holi does not fall on the same day every year because Hindus follow the "lunar" calendar, which is based on the phases of the moon.
Holi falls on "Purnima".
It is all about welcoming the new crops and colourful flowers that start to bloom in Spring. It is also seen as an opportunity for friends to put aside their differences and reconnect with warmth and affection.

Purnima means:
Full Moon

The natural colours of Holi

Holi is celebrated by spreading vibrant colours of Spring among friends and family in the form of coloured powder called, "gulal", that people playfully sprinkle on each other. Gulal is traditionally made with flowers, but nowadays with cornflower and food colouring.

Farmers have had a great crop, Flowers begin to bloom and sway.

The air is warmer and friends all gather with colours they celebrate away.

The natural colours of Holi

Do you know where the coloured powders called Gulal, come from?
The pretty colourful flowers of Spring are gathered much in advance to make all our Holi colours. The flowers are left to dry, and then they are pressed into fine powder.

Gulal is pronounced Goo-lal

Since Holi is played with bright colours, you must wear clothes that you do not mind spoiling! Or you can wear special white clothes - the bright Holi colours show best on these.

Red signifies love. Hibiscus flowers or Roses are best for a vibrant red hue.

Yellow is happiness and hope. Bright Marigolds are great for making yellow gulal.

Orange stands for enthusiasm. The Flame of the Forest, also known as 'Tesu' is the most popular for the orange colour.

Green signifies life and freshness. Fresh neem leaves make a green gulal.

Purple is a royal colour. Lavender, orchids, and lilacs can be used to make a purple-coloured gulal.

Blue is calm. The Iris is a flower that can give you a natural cool blue.

Holi celebrations across the land

Here are some of the ways Holi is celebrated across different states of India:

South India

Manjal Kuli

Celebrated in Kerela, mainly by the Malayali community, a beautiful dance ritual takes place in the temples, backed by music and drums. Turmeric-coloured water is sprayed towards the north and a special tree is taken to the shrine, symbolising another legend of Goddess Durga's victory over the demons.

North India

Lathmar Holi
Holi is celebrated in a unique way in Barsana and Nandgaon with the wives playfully chasing away their husbands with 'lathis' (sticks). The husbands apologise to their wives, and they all laugh and cheer together!

Khadi Holi
In Kumaoni, Uttarakhand, revellers wear traditional handwoven clothes and celebrate Holi with music, songs and dance. The comfortable khadi clothing is coloured with various hues, by people celebrating the festival of colours.

Hola Mohalla
This is known as 'warrior Holi' and is celebrated in Punjab with martial arts performances and horse-riding tricks on the day before Holi. The Sikh community in Northern India celebrate Holi with passion and pride!

East India

Dol Jatra
In West Bengal, Holi is all about welcoming Spring and the revellers wear shades of orange and spray one another with coloured water with a Pichkari. No Indian festival is complete without music, dance and delicacies. Holi is no exception. People enjoy snacks like gu-ji-yas, dahi-vada, la-doos, buttermilk, than-da-i and bhang.

Phaguwa
As the drums beat loudly, men and women dance in a unique fashion. The men wear turbans and women dress up in colourful clothes. Lighting the Holika is an important part of the celebrations in Bihar.

Yaosang
A traditional folk dance is performed, where boys and girls hold hands and dance in a circle to celebrate Holi in Manipur. The dance is also called the 'moonlight dance' as it is performed at night. Here, Holi is celebrated for six days with folk dances and songs.

West India

Shigmo
In Goa, people paint their faces and set out on the streets to celebrate this joyous occasion. Here, Spring is celebrated with farmers performing traditional folk and street dances.

Rang Panchami
Fragrant red coloured gulal is thrown around in Maharashtra while people celebrate with gau abandon. Holi is celebrated on the fifth day after Holika Dahan.

Royal Holi
With a sacred and spiritual approach, locals in Rajasthan light bonfires to be rid of evil spirits and mark Holika Dahan.

Activity: Connect the Colours

Can you connect the correct colour with the corresponding Hindi word?

RED	GULABI
WHITE	NEELA
BLUE	LAAL
YELLOW	HARA
ORANGE	KALA
PINK	PEELA
GREEN	SAFAED
BLACK	NARANGI

Activity: Holi Word Search

Can you find the words you learnt in the book? Good Luck!

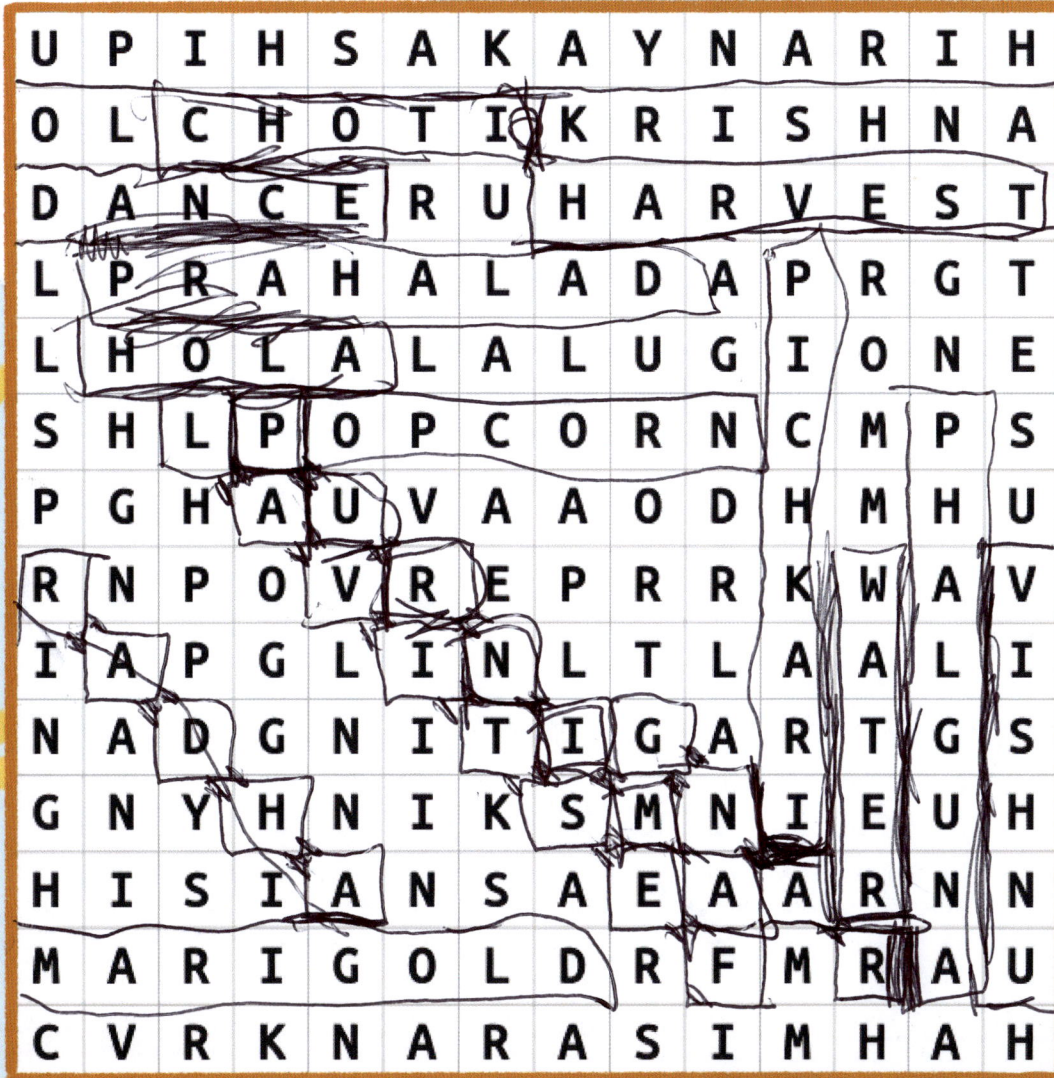

U	P	I	H	S	A	K	A	Y	N	A	R	I	H
O	L	C	H	O	T	I	K	R	I	S	H	N	A
D	A	N	C	E	R	U	H	A	R	V	E	S	T
L	P	R	A	H	A	L	A	D	A	P	R	G	T
L	H	O	L	A	L	A	L	U	G	I	O	N	E
S	H	L	P	O	P	C	O	R	N	C	M	P	S
P	G	H	A	U	V	A	A	O	D	H	M	H	U
R	N	P	O	V	R	E	P	R	R	K	W	A	V
I	A	P	G	L	I	N	L	T	L	A	A	L	I
N	A	D	G	N	I	T	I	G	A	R	T	G	S
G	N	Y	H	N	I	K	S	M	N	I	E	U	H
H	I	S	I	A	N	S	A	E	A	A	R	N	N
M	A	R	I	G	O	L	D	R	F	M	R	A	U
C	V	R	K	N	A	R	A	S	I	M	H	A	H

- ✓ DANCE
- ✓ FESTIVAL
- ✓ RANG
- ✓ PHALGUNA
- ✓ PICHKARI
- HIRANYAKASHIPU
- VISHNU ✓
- WATER ✓
- HOLA
- MARIGOLD
- PRAHALAD
- POPCORN
- RADHA ✓
- CHOTI ✓
- PURNIMA
- NARASIMHA
- HOLIKA
- SPRING
- HARVEST ✓
- SING
- LOVE
- TESU
- GULAL
- KRISHNA

Answers on last page.

The Delicacies of Holi

Holi is a time for fun with friends, family and food!
Do you recognise any of these delicious delicacies?

Thandai – A milk drink filled with cinnamon, cardamon and saffron

Ghewar – is like a big j-lebi. It is a sweet thin string wrapped in a circle

Badam (Almond) Phirni – is a sweet creamy dessert

Puran-poli – a sweet paratha filled with jaggery and lentils

Malpua – an Indian pancake with rab-a-di (an Indian sweet cream sauce)

Gujiya – It's like a sweet samosa

Dahi Bhalla – refreshing curd with spices and tamarind chutneys

Holi greetings – Yay! It's Holi!

Here is a lovely song you can learn:

Holi aai,
Holi aai,
Holi aai ray!
Rang la-gaa -o
Khushi mana-o
Holi aai ray!

This means:
Holi has come!
Let's play with colour
and celebrate with joy!

Go to
www.magicofindea.org
or scan the QR code to
hear the song and sing
along!

Learn this song and one more on magicofindia.org.

Here are some joyful greetings you can say with your friends to celebrate Holi!

Happy Holi!

Holi Hai!
(It is Holi!)

Rang k-han hai?
(Where are the colours?)

Chalo – lets play Holi!
(Come on, lets play Holi!)

Answers:

Did you get them all right?

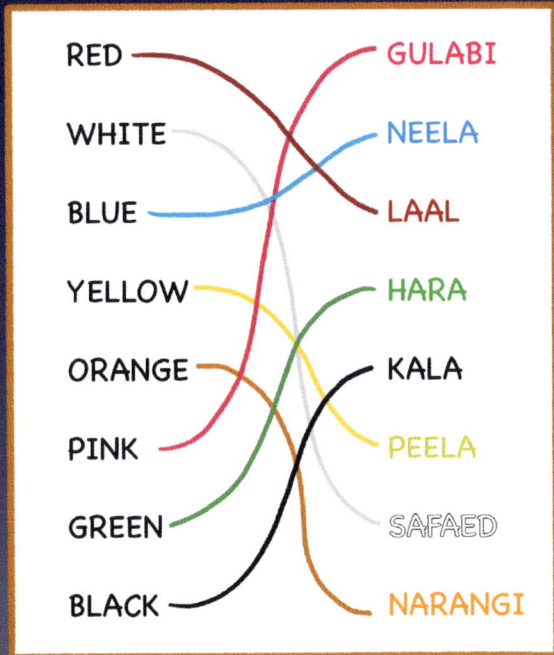

RED	GULABI
WHITE	NEELA
BLUE	LAAL
YELLOW	HARA
ORANGE	KALA
PINK	PEELA
GREEN	SAFAED
BLACK	NARANGI

```
U P I H S A K A Y N A R I H
O L C H O T I K R I S H N A
D A N C E R U H A R V E S T
L P R A H A L A D A P R G T
L H O L A L A L U G I O N E
S H L P O P C O R N C M P S
P G H A U V A A O D H M H U
R N P O V R E P R R K W A V
I A P G L I N L T L A A L I
N A D G N I T I G A R T G S
G N Y H N I K S M N I E U H
H I S I A N S A E A A R N N
M A R I G O L D R F M R A U
C V R K N A R A S I M H A H
```

Activity: Rainbow Butterflies

Cut out the butterfly shapes. Colour them in with as many colours as you can! Stick them together in the middle with some glue and stick them on a wall or hang with string.

Cut along the dotted line

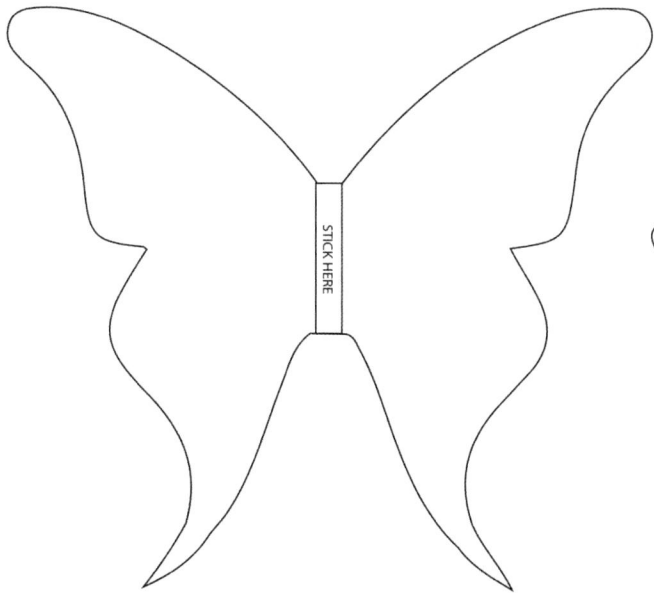

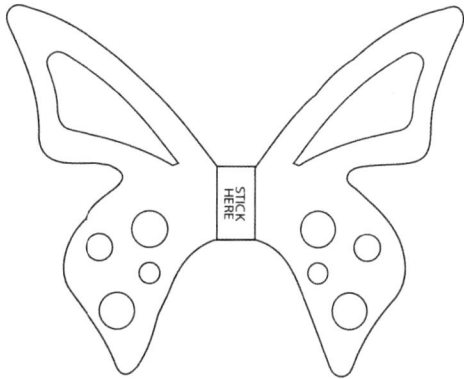

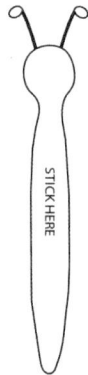

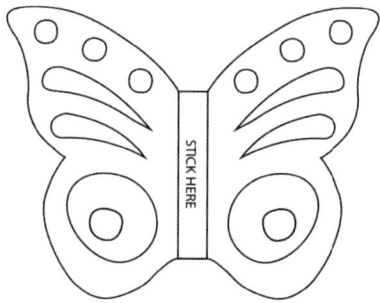

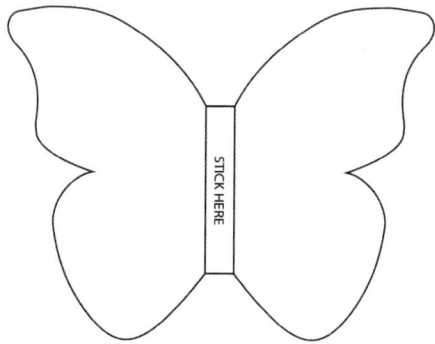

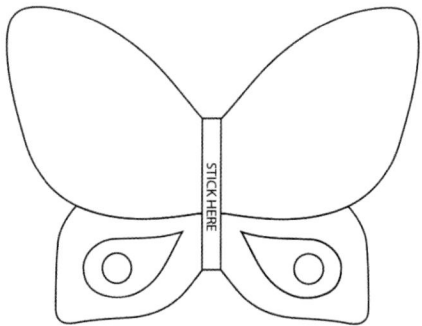

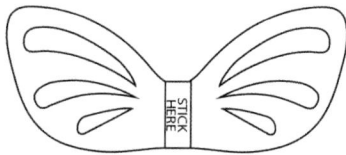

Printed in Great Britain
by Amazon

38280350R00018